The Drive To Monetize ME

William [Bill] Money

Copyright © 2025

All rights reserved.

No part of this book may be reproduced, or stored in a retrieval system, or transmitted in any form or by any means, electronic, mechanical, photocopying, recording, or otherwise, without express written permission of the publisher.

Printed and/ or distributed (Electronically) in the United States of America and abroad by right of corporate partnership and agreements on file with publishing entity 4FM Publishing Group.

Bill Money - 4FM Publishing

FUEL

If I may be so bold to declare. Today is a good day!

In fact, let me say, every day is good. A good day to make a profitable honest living. To provide for yourself and your family... Today, in my estimation, is the perfect day to discuss You and I - ME. The man who grew up believing in a principle – Money by any means.

Some would rather eat than starve (meaning they can easily accept what comes), I would rather feast and be full than beg for a dime (meaning , I'm going to take all you can give me plus some when necessary).

Blame it on Reaganomics since that's the frame of time I was raised in. Or perhaps it was the rappers I found fascinating. Regardless, I would rather eat well as the scripture says, "money answereth all things" than hope, much less beg, for anyone to feed me.

This world, in my mind, owes me that much and I'm going to damn sure collect! Figure out how to get it!

Forgive me, if that hint of honesty seems a bit much to you. It was a necessity if not slightly appropriate because. This thought, this book is something of a monologue; with dialogue tendencies; principles.

It's an exchange with you, my paying partners, in this publishing arena. With me providing the inspiration; information, whatever I can give/ explain about earnings.

IGNITION

You see, this book is something of an anomaly. I intended it to be motivational and spiritually nourishing. Most of all though I intend it to be lucrative and beneficial to ME. To you as well dear reader don't misunderstand!

I don't want you to think you wasted your money. Or got a hold of something that's only meant to line my pockets so to speak.

This book is about the recognition and power of potential. How and why it can and should be used to effectively make us better, more successful people. You and I.

Or, at least, successful past living and hoping/ wishing for something better..

This book is about finding, taking; making the most of an opportunity. Seizing the day, especially while you're young and best able to grow and make use of the principles to make us (old me and you) independently wealthy individuals.

MOMENTUM

The hope is. Indeed my prayer is...

This seed produces a greater harvest of fruit for you and your people to enjoy and multiply. This, or rather, these words are meant to encourage and remind you of the power and ability of YOU to be successful in all things through Him, He who designed you!

In Christ name,
AMEN

Contents

FUEL	5
IGNITION	9
MOMENTUM	11
Work Is Work	17
[The Gift and The Treasure]	23
[The Give and Take Tree]	27
The Value I Have	31
[Understanding You and Your Value]	36
Becoming - Immeasurable	43
[Determination]	47
[The Growth of WE]	49

Guides and Guidance	53
[The Right Part for Fit]	59
The Drive – More Than Others Define	63
[More]	67
Gratitude	73
More From 4FM Publishing	75
Biography	77

"The only way to do great work is to love what you do."

– Steve Jobs.

Principle 1
Work Is Work

> *You will have to work hard for a long time before you have any food to eat. You will do this for your whole life until you die.*
>
> GENESIS 3:19 (EASY)

I have a little something I'd like to confess before we get under way. It took me a while to get to this moment. There was simply no one who could explain to me the intricacies of me. How best to better my steps and how to gain, accomplish the mission of wealth. There were many who tried to explain the benefits and those who tried to mold me into their idea of mature and grown. But very few who knew or could explain a successful me, to me.

Specifically, they couldn't teach or didn't speak in a language or conversation I could understand. So I essentially became a hybrid, a blend of people, of whom I picked and chose for myself what worked for me in the moment.

If I could explain it... That is kind of a running theme in life but it isn't the best way to grow wealth unless you happen to be born with a headstart. Or silver spoon as they say. But that's for another book...

In beginning this conversation, this book. It's as much about me as it is a blueprint for you. I had to reach a discovery, as we all do, on my own and in my own time. The latter, presenting me a reminder that wealth and life comes from a decision, my decisions on - allocating resources and putting talents to use, while they're useful.

The drive to monetize me was not, is not, simply about wealth building or money generation. It's about gathering the harvest. Beyond something falling into my lap, it's about using, that is, putting certain tools to work for me. The equipment package I've already been loaded with.

It's a hint of an extract of something T.D. Jakes said that

sticks with me, to this day.

In one of his messages, relaying a time when he was just getting started and needed resources (to paraphrase the story). To feed his young family and build a burgeoning ministry. "I started digging trenches, cutting grass, and frying chicken. Before I started writing plays and books and other things... I begin to work at it, for little or nothing."

The point being. I had to learn to work at it. Not according to what or how the system says it should be done. But according to my wants (I wanted to please God). He calls it being faithful over the little until God elevates you to much.

My reality was, I'd been neglecting the opportunity to be fruitful and multiply and just trying to be fruitful or multiply (the world's way). To see the multiplication I desired in my life. I had to employ the fruits of the spirit that is within me. Because I haven't or hadn't to this point, employed all the tools in my arsenal, so to speak, on my behalf. I had a full trough of misery and regret anytime a storm came instead of a continuous winning formula (producing for me); Today though, that changes!

The Drive To Monetize ME

The drive for me is about hunger. It's about self reflection. But more than anything, it's about improving the life I've been given while I'm given it and helping you to improve yours as well.

This group of principles, or collection of ideas, while centered on a simple thought, is more than your average get rich quick scheme. There are no pyramids involved. It's about a change in mindset and attitude. An alternative pursuit if you will.

It's about having, developing; growing something organically. That is naturally a part of every man, woman and being. And it's available for everybody even if some neglect to use it or even acknowledge it. Choosing rather a shorter means to accomplish things. The larger idea, I won't even delve into. In this case it would only serve to hinder things. The definitive is... work is work. The truth is... The fact is...

Work produces what you produce from it!

Work is WORK!

Now myself, I've never really had a problem with the concept of work. I would even say, I rather enjoy it. I like to work!

In actuality most people, if asked, would say they enjoy the activity; they don't mind the "being active"of work. Some might even say they like the work they do, as do I! The exercise of pursuing what they're good at. And in some cases excel at... You can make a lucrative living doing it, but more than that it is well (beneficial healthwise) with them, us. The thing though that causes the attitude. The thing most fight or don't like is - having to work. Being compelled to (work) do something to support a certain lifestyle or to meet some expectations. This is what causes people the most insane amounts of stress and discomfort. You add to that the labels and scale some affix to jobs, even under the guise of organization, and the discomfort of work increases.

This happens primarily because many don't understand work is work. Managers, supervisors, employees agree that work is work. But they forget - Work is Work! Work has meaning! Work has purpose! Work has benefit! Meaning it's beneficial to you (both parties). It even has benefits (although different meaning, for both parties).

Work is not meant to be work (driving and stressful) it's meant to be (work) an activity you may or may not do for money, but to be thoroughly enjoyed by everyone on all levels.

[The Gift and The Treasure]

Having explained the simple nature of work, the activity and demands of. Let's turn the focus to the ability to work - to perform the activity or activities in question.

Natural talent being a part of an expression of a design feature of me and you - Humanity. A gift! The natural ability or rather abilities inherent in every being. Put in place to edify the one who gave them and the one who uses them. But I won't dwell on that.

As gifted, as talented, as an individual may be, the blessing (of we) is in the effort. Excellence requires effort. And even more it is the very attribute that is vitally important to proving faith and getting us paid.

There is little, other than our own ideals; that separate us and the value of a job. The fact is all things have to get done, and somebody will ultimately do them. Why not me, if I have a certain set of skills. Put tools to work! Be fruitful - and multiply!

There are two parts of the equation, yet both are the command. Be fruitful. For a time all things may function with or without you. But to add multiplication, you have to be smart and employ all the necessary parts (of everything) to make the engine work. I say again. The reality is - work is work.

Work is not title specific or gender important, if something needs to be done; somebody has to do it. It's a most basic principle of the position of a worker. You perform or have a job somebody created. Your abilities answer a need. This makes you an integral part of the engine cycle. But it also invites a secondary question. What is the payoff? What many view as the earnings potential question. People work to earn.

People expend effort to affect pay. They expect to be paid, to reach their payoff number. That is the primary motivator now. But it wasn't or isn't the way the equation goes. Be fruitful and multiply! The primary reason has changed. And it really needs to be changed back.

Work is still work (effort). But now the motivation to provide it is. What's in it for me? How much do I earn? Depending on this, is how much I will extend myself in effort. Money has become the primary influence of wealth building. Replacing the idea of "get it done because it needs to be done."

This doesn't mean though money is the whole issue. Like it or not, money is an appreciable tool, a measure by which people live. It can add to free exchange. It helps keep the engine running. So its value is invaluable. However the influence it has - has created an issue. Very few now will venture to perform a service they can easily do because of the influence of money. Work has become an issue because the view of benefits has been supplanted. If it doesn't pay me "exponentially" why should I do it?

People begin businesses and expect immediate returns. Many without ever considering first to establish a value, then receive the reward. Now it's income – income - income, for as little as I can give. Even when working for employers the idea is earnings first then we'll negotiate the work.

It's an attempt to defy a principle that ultimately proves true anyway. Work is work.
All jobs matter. All work pays. The benefits though aren't the most valuable thing. The value is in seizing the opportunity and doing things just because something needs to be done.

This thought is at the heart of these principles and why working to monetize you is more than just what we earn. It's more easily summed as this. If you want more you have to give more.

[The Give and Take Tree]

Work has to start with a why not me attitude. Whether an employer, employee, or budding opportunist, why not you? If I can do it. So can ou! Do it and get it done!

You're looking to boost your financial health. You're looking to earn a steady income. You're looking at the bottom line. How dare you say something is beneath you? If it needs to be done and you know how to do it. Do it! Change your attitude!

Pick up a why not you attitude! Why not you, or why don't you go the extra mile and see the earnings it brings you.
You'll be amazed I think. The more indispensable you become, the more invaluable you and your service are. The more then there is an opportunity for you to profit. Soon you'll find yourself in the best asset category. The "appreciable asset!" The place where the real money comes. But I'm getting ahead of myself.

One of the reasons I'm (crafting this message) putting

together this information is a work requirement. Work commands I write, as an author, so I write. I need money, so I produce. And yet, this is also something I thoroughly enjoy doing. Providing a text for you to think about, consider and hopefully put to practice.

I'm reminded of a lesson or rather a thought taught to Adam and Eve. Genesis 3:19 *[EASY] You will have to work hard for a long time before you have any food to eat. You will do this for your whole life until you die. Then you will return into the ground. That is where you came from. I made you from the soil of the ground, and you will become soil again.'* The New King James says it like this. *[NKJV] In the sweat of your face you shall eat bread Till you return to the ground, For out of it you were taken; For dust you are, And to dust you shall return."*

That in itself establishes something the old people said. "Easy come easy go." To earn money fast or to earn money long you still have to work at it. And working at it means "ten percent inspiration and ninety percent perspiration." There are no shortcuts to sustained success.

You'll see this a little better in the next section.

The Economics of Work: Provision & Value

Because of the way some view work (the activity and benefits of), there is a need to explain an important provision or motivation in work (necessity and behavior). 2nd Thessalonians 3:10 – (paraphrased) you don't work you don't eat.

The question of importance to you then is. How hungry are you?

Bill Money

Principle 2
The Value I Have

> *So do not be afraid of those people who are against you. You are more valuable to God than many little birds.*
>
> MATTHEW 10:31 (EASY)

With a more firm grasp on what I'll call, sweat equity. I need to further explain something about my understanding of value and worth. In the words made famous by the late Jesse Jackson, "I am Somebody."

With that as a more complete introduction of me and embracing the principle of work. We can now begin to look into the motivations or motivating factors; the fuel driving the automobile of work or work habits.

Keep in mind though this statement at all times. Remember Your Worth!

With that, we have a clearer vantage to begin examining the earnings or pay side of the conversation. The "how much and how soon" does this "work" pay? Or, when does this job actually begin to pay me? It's a fairly simple question and even evolves, at a point, to a simple answer to the question, does work pay? The answer is simply, yes! Work pays! Work has benefits! Yet the benefits are self determined. With a qualifier. There are no actual numerical numbers you can factor into it. The value or valuation varies, perhaps that might sound better.

It is based primarily on the answer you provide to three points. These points are the direct result of knowing and believing in myself. Which leads us to a more indepth view of our persons, but first. Let me convey this mentality.

- Work is work
- Work benefits the worker
- Work is an opportunity (for greater or greatness)

Our personal motivations and characters, the things that cause you and I; us to pursue goals is what makes us unique and it also makes it hard to determine value for work. Hard to put an actual number to it. Shout out to the INDEED commercial. LOL! (a competitive number) This makes it imperative that we look, for a moment, to brush past the money or profit motivation into an exam of how you see yourself.

Some would refer to this line of thinking as determining your healthy self image. I'd like to think of it as a correct personal image. An assessment if you will. The picture of which man (this includes women) was made and which man stands when we look in the mirror.

The image is described as saying. We're made to prosper. To be fruitful and multiply. We're designed or instructed to fit the exact specifications of our creator, to be a literal compliment (to him and one another I might add). This means our primary focus, our numbered driver, the one thing we need to know (as an individual) is. I Have Value! An established worth in His eyes and therefore my eyes.

There is no more powerful statement of wealth than recognizing the fact. I am valuable, knowing - I have value!

That had been taken from me for a time. To one degree or another I've had to remind myself over the years, in the words of Mr. Jackson, "I am somebody!"

For all the depression and devaluation… We all tend to neglect this thought, especially in our youth. Lacking in appreciation of responsibility. And it's something that will hinder the execution (Implementation) of our strategy, of work and accomplishment, when we're not taught this part early. I have value!

More than anything. It will impact tomorrow's expectation if I can't see it and say it. Especially when tough times, or struggles or setbacks occur because negativity breeds negativity just as positive thinking breeds positive…

We need to, then in that moment, remember and remind ourselves. Add a quick strengthening boost, I say. According to my belief in the Creator's account. I am, we are, wonderfully made. Not simply a summation of our parents or ancestors. Not simply a product of our environments. You! I am special! I AM SOMEBODY!

I have certain materials, certain experience; that to me - create or add to my being. They add to my composite, my composition, to me. These things add to my value. I have the gifts or seed information to bear a real - special, specialized yet tasty fruit.
To be what, if you believe, my creator ascribed to me.

These same things have marketability. They make me have worth. They have and add value to me. And with them in my possession it is thereby deemed. I HAVE VALUE - greater than some might think.
If you need to discover this or rediscover this, it's important to know and be firm on. I am precious! I am valuable! I am uniquely and wonderfully designed and made!
I say again, "Remember your worth!"

Spiritually, intrinsically, naturally; inherently – I have a place in this world. I have a value (not just monetarily). I have a net worth - a set worth. That's what makes hearing, absorbing, these words all the more powerful. Before we begin to assign a numerical value to our work. Before we even begin to monetize myself; I had to think about who I am in His sight.

Then I could assign a numerical value to me and my work. At this point so can you, on our journey to wealth. It's important to know at least the basic financial (makeup) of you. You have value! So too does your work!

Now we can begin to understand (examine) what makes us important to the business world, to our environment - to the wealth gathering community.

[Understanding You and Your Value]

For that exercise we need to begin with these three thoughts.

- What do I know?
- What can I do?
- What am I willing to do?

What some might call finding confidence in creativity

or assigning currency to assertiveness, I call assessing the state of where you are before and where you seek to go. To determine the exact location of where you are on the road to success.

Are you a business owner seeking to grow his/ her base? Are you a creative thinker looking to get your art an audience? Are you a single something trying to get or be a part of something bigger than you? You have to first come to the realization of this. I bring something to the table. Like Jesse said, "I AM SOMEBODY!"

The world may assign a number as easy as a credit score. But that doesn't mean it establishes you or your worth.. A friend once said, Joe Campbell, "I am more than others define."

Others might wish to classify you according to their definition of living or having success. But ultimately it's you, who gets to define the value of you, the asset. You set your value. You determine the value of your work

To put it in earning terms. To begin to earn income, or

hold a job, you have to know the value you possess in order to influence your bargaining power. Before progressing to what does this job pay? Ask yourself, what worth am I bringing to the job or position?

Allow me to preface this thought with a note. Everything has value to everyone. But not everybody assigns the same value to everything.

So don't think of this as saying you should go and demand a substantial increase in pay simply because you feel you're invaluable to your company. What I'm actually saying is, knowing your value, if you desire to earn more - allows you to be more.

Whether you're starting your own business or creating work under someone else's banner the key to earning more is knowing more or doing more or becoming more. All work (the numerical value of) fits into three categories. From the first assessment of I Have Value - to becoming an indispensable, irreplaceable asset.

Before you can proceed to negotiate, this is what I'm worth – this is what I make myself worth. Take a perspective on these things.

Your education. Your experience. Your talents or God gifted ability.

You need to know these things to assess what you're willing to do to benefit you. To make you money - fast or slow or more. You have to use these criteria to define you. And then others can read your book. If you don't then others surely will attempt to. And assign you random numbers which over time you'll likely land on unhappy with.

I should expound on that but first I have to ask. What skills or predilections do you have? What special thing have you picked up along the way? These are things that make you marketable regardless of age. And finally, what are you willing to do? Sometimes life throws us curveballs and you can wind up in an alternate career choice. Yet God can make it work. You can make it work. This doesn't alter (determine) your wealth building journey's effectiveness unless you let it.

That's part of the recognition of, you get what you deserve

when you deserve what you get. Your real, not your inherent value is predetermined but we, I had to learn it.

I'm reminded of a statement from the text of God... whatever your hand finds to do, DO IT! To the best of your ability! With all you are, your dedication
This is the testament of your faith and belief in the statement I have Value!
If you? When you know who you are. You can begin to make strategic investments in a set, read that, real strategy to build a better life. To monetize ME!

Weigh these things before you go any further.

- What do I know - about life, about work, about anything...?
- What can I do - in life, for work,, to earn a living...?
- What am I willing to do - to get better, to be better, to improve myself; to find my, all my, God given skills...?

These questions or rather the answers to them will lead us

directly into the next idea of becoming invaluable. But we won't jump too far too fast. Let's first get an idea of. What is MY NUMBER?

What determination have I made about where I want to go or be wealth wise? Take a moment here! Don't rush the thought!

Do you have an image in focus?

Now I think you're sufficiently prepared for the next stage of our journey.

The Appreciating Part of ME

This area is the best and most profiting part of the pursuit of who I am as a being and who I'm meant to be. Now that you've discovered your value let's turn it and you into more. (Luke 12:7 [EASY] - So do not be afraid of those people who are against you. You are more valuable to God than many little birds.)

Bill Money

Principle 3

Becoming - Immeasurable

> *And here is how to measure it—the greatest love is shown when a person lays down his life for his friends;*
>
> JOHN 15:13 (TLB)

At this point I'd like to introduce a term you may or may not be familiar with. The "indispensable tool or invaluable resource."

Usually associated with something you can't easily put a price on or assign a value to. This is seemingly the highest compliment that can be offered of a person, place or thing. To say, I cannot put a measurable number to your benefit, either to me or my company.

Whether the discussion is information, your knowledge; or technical proficiency, your expertise. To be crowned an invaluable resource is as great a plateau as saying expressly - I can't do it without you. You are the perfect compliment to me for my success. It means you're doing something good; something right. It means something on every level except when you're trying to actually hit a number - to be paid.

This is where the definition of work changes. The meaning to you and I is switched here. Because the expectation shifts from what do I know and what can I do? The focus becomes how is having me around advantageous to me - or them?

Typically an employer prices the work, and the amount of value perceived in the work. But most try to limit or avoid altogether the conversation of pricing the person or personnel. The reasons are numerous but it can be summed into a saying, the elimination of personal feelings and ideology.

That, however, is a washout to me. I'd rather believe it is, as a, critical element to monetizing me or you - good to know what people think about you monetarily speaking.

In the corporate environment and strategic thinking, you cannot put a limit on people without putting a limit on people. You can avoid at all cost considering individuals when valuing the measurement of performance in general. In terms of formulas and equations, I mean. However, to present the illusion or image of fairness, you must leave the personal out of it. Even though the individual, his or her effort, is the force that makes the engine go!

Because of this the first two principles are made more important. To help individuals compensate or rather refocus their thinking. For when their work (effort) is overlooked or disregarded or in extreme cases minimized. Especially knowing that, in the end, it may ruin the performance narrative of good work. The being excellent at what you do, or work.

That being said.

This effort will hopefully change minds and attitudes of people - resources. Because I believe we can all prosper and succeed. We can all thrive and bear fruit to our level as designed. The key is getting the most out of us - the individual. That is getting us to recognize we are the asset. We are the "invaluable resource". As an engine doesn't go without lube and gas as well as parts. This engine can not go without its parts and fuel, without aligning some things to work better and produce more (that is actual) horse power or people power. This engine doesn't run right without You! That's the facts of things.

[Determination]

In monetizing efforts you want to strive for the ultimate goal, which is to become an invaluable tool; an invaluable resource. However this isn't the end of the discussion because as life teaches us. Tools get used and many can be replaced. So the peak of performance or the optimum goal is to transform your approach to one where people appreciate your value. Appreciate your work, dedication, professionalism... Appreciate you i.e. having you around!

Becoming an indispensable part... Making yourself an irreplaceable resource rather than simply an asset. Being good (at your job) is as good a first step as any. But, to be honest, it can also be problematic unless you understand how making you and your work an appreciable asset works for you.

Let me say it this way. The difference between people seeing or saying, you're appreciated and you're invaluable is most of the time people offer the compliment of "indispensable" to or for services they don't actually pay for.

Usually! That is they don't or didn't have to invest anything for them to benefit. In essence they earn from your abilities without incurring the cost. Now there's nothing wrong with that in and of itself. Unless you're seeking a mutual exchange of benefits. Which the drive is absolutely about!

I help you, to help me! You're helping them gain and strengthen their bottom line to effectively increase your bottom line. That's the place where incentives like raises and bonuses come from. And they can help determine whether you're identified as an asset, an invaluable asset or an appreciable asset. Somebody who's getting paid and promoted within and without the company.

Again though, let's not get sidetracked. When your goal is to determine your present value with an eye towards future earnings. You have to be accurate in assessing yourself. Be truthful and as specific as possible with where you stand in the work department. Be real and then you can begin setting value and determine growth strategies. This is most important because your mindset, your focus has to be on seeing yourself as not only valuable but as an appreciating asset. This means a dedicated (to working) individual. With a dedication, not only an expectancy, of reaching wages or a salary commensurate with - compensation matching your actual perceived value.

This also means forming an intent.

[The Growth of WE]

I intend to grow with or in the place I'm planted. I'm here to see and aid the company's growth for my growth, our growth. This is a good working relationship and in actuality a partnership of cooperation. This is something to be encouraged in life as well as business and is important for fruit bearing operations. You have to have a partner. Which means you have to be a partner!

Whether each partner later agrees on their aftermarket; individual value then becomes almost irrelevant, the focus is on the one goal – monetizing the (all) assets. Or, at the least, creating a value of all the costs involved before becoming an invaluable resource.

A great example of this is social media. Social networks have the value they have because people place a value on being social. People "business owners" need people to buy their products. The best place to sell your products to people is where people are. By creating this place social networks get paid essentially from all sides.

They have become an "invaluable resource" that also happens to be an "appreciable asset". You can do the same.

Your effort can get you paid. It's only a matter of how you direct it. More to point it's how, where and what - you direct it on.

This brings to mind the INDEED commercial. When the guy wants to know the salary, the lady says the salary offered is competitive. If I ask you to put a number to it, the guy says. It would be a competitive number, is her response. Some people will do anything not to fix value to a position or person.

That's almost like the minimum wage in business. If you can get somebody to do it for the minimum, why pay fair or even the maximum? It's not your "responsibility" to know their value and evaluated self worth.

To be completely honest in my thoughts here. People tend to want something for nothing if they can get it. But the reality is. Everything costs. Everything costs everybody something!

A popular thought says, "when they go low we go high" meaning take the high road essentially. In Business however that thought is reversed or better said doesn't so much apply.

When others go high (price) or earnings expectations for themselves, according to their perceived value. There's always somebody willing to go lower to beat them out for the job. That's how most successful businesses are built and business owners think. But, what if value was more realistic? As I said - there's three things I want you to consider.

- What I know how to do...
- What I can do. Learn expeditiously on the job...

- What I'm willing to do. Even if it means lowering my perceived value (asking price)

Choosing a Direction

How, where and what gets you paid the fastest? What's the best choice of employment and work? It's difficult to say without knowing you. I know what works for me and what can work for you if you put in the practice but that means being hungry. So I ask?

How hungry are you? Remember, you don't work, you won't eat!

Principle 4

Guides and Guidance

> *This is exactly why, while with you, we commanded you: "Anyone not willing to work shouldn't get to eat!"*
>
> 2nd THESSALONIANS 3:10 (VOICE)

This is the one principle I turn to most often. As it keeps the attention on me in a self surveying sense. It relays a fact that I was slow to embrace at first. But when I did, it reignited a passion in me that had long laid dormant. The passion being to know myself and remind myself of who I am! Who I'm meant to be! What makes me, me! I'm made of stern stuff! The verse from Isaiah applies to me (51:1). I can do what I set my mind to do! Part of which is what I'm doing here, monetizing me. Notwithstanding that, let me say, what works for me may not (work) be for everybody. That doesn't mean it doesn't work. That's why I emphasize knowing yourself and where you stand in the process.

Having said all that. Let's get back to business!

There are unlimited opportunities in the world to make a life; a financial living. I may be dating myself here. A quick look through the classifieds. Viewing job boards, scouring the internet – there is no shortage of work opportunities available. There is no shortage of people offering career advice and personal counseling. All these things though have a price. All these things have a cost. But they also share a unique common feature or should I say goal.

They're each out to capture your capital. The funds from your putting your earning potential into action. They're after your money! So too are we to some degree - to be transparent. Yet, our real motivation is trying to voice and focusing our efforts towards helping to develop a stronger more well rounded workforce for lack of a better term. A more aware and diverse population group more in touch with the principled people of God's creation. If you can't tell yet, I'm a Christ believer.

We're trying to help people be better as well as earn more;

at least reach their highest earning potential (in something they love or enjoy doing). Communicating how to eat well and be well while doing the work of working. Something that's possible beyond just settling for a paycheck. That's our real motivation.

I believe we can be more and receive more; definitely produce more. The key is to find the balance within. The rhythm and harmony of life that makes us as individuals, grow.

The good thing is employers are looking for these people. It could be said even people are looking for these individuals to hang around. They want people who will come to work and work (enjoyably). They pay advertisers or post jobs to draw people looking for work. The people hosting these advertisements want people, traffic to see the jobs and whatever else they offer. All these individual things are a part of the partnership associated with being successful at work: They're doing what gives them purpose.

They're helping you to form a relationship. A cooperative if you will, one of trading your invaluable resources or appreciable assets for their monetary resource; or financial gain. The main goal, the shared pursuit, is to monetize things. Be it you, traffic, even products. It could be as simple as buy or sell. But to pursue the where, how, what will get you paid (fastest) depends on where you see yourself in the equation.

That is what I call your prime direction. Or should I say the most premium course for you to pursue.

If you still aren't sure what you know, take a minute or two and get to know you! And then you can direct your energy into what works for you in your situation. Some of the things you may find even crossover and provide multiple opportunities for you. This is your opportunity to bear fruit, or reproduce. The knowledge and skill being the root of your tree, now you're prepared to put something out there to be consumed. In our case it's reap the financial gains, rewards of your labor efforts. As I said, natural talents and predilections play a role in your decision, but in either case things need to be honed to reap the maximum amount.

For a more personal example, let me take a second to tell my story more fully.

I'm a writer amongst my many other interests, other talents. And to pursue the career as a writer; I'm required to have a set of skills that I didn't necessarily have or hone at first. Yet I had them. I know people and although somewhat an introvert, I see people. I understand or better said, understood the connection of people in relation to the world. So my pursuit of a writing communicating interest was natural to me. And although tedious at times; it never stops being enjoyable. I can never not see the joy in penning or typing something; anything. This same spirit can apply to whatever job you're in or you choose. Whether it be sports or construction. Your personal blueprint (makeup) is your road map for the possibility of success for you!

The execution or acting on it (that's what we call faith). Being faithful and committed to the vision you drive by. This is what actually produces the fruit in your life. That's where your wealth and more is hidden.

You can't be out of place and out of time and not be found, at the same time, out of character. At least that's where I was before deciding to examine myself and my steps. Taking a hard look into the opportunities I had. Those I had taken advantage of and those I didn't.

Lest I forget, however. There's room for a third part of the equation which we'll delve more deeply into in the final part of this discussion. Suffice it to say now. The, what am I willing to do, part. Beyond what I know or learn of myself. What am I willing to do to contribute to my success?

That's sorting you have to ask yourself. But that involves a deeper knowledge of you and honestly some time with your creator. What I mean is you can skip steps in some cases and go straight to what I'm willing to do for money. Come up with an answer and pursue it. And sometimes it yields great fruit, I can't lie. It works. However I warn you it can be quite costly. The weights' not always worth the wait or the headache of making a bad choice. So let's instead focus on the general motivations.

[The Right Part for Fit]

If I'm looking for a job or career opportunity, then beginning with my value, I respond to an advertisement. My goal is to then show myself first capable and then an invaluable resource or asset to the person hiring. But that's not the end. I have to then prove and continue to prove myself invaluable throughout my tenure with that employer to earn more.

The same is true whether you're looking for the next salary bump or trying to find a way to supplement your pay on your own. This opportunity has to be or become your opportunity to develop something beneficial to us all. That beneficial product is a better you.

In other words, the partnership has to be an actual partner role for both parties to draw on and in the most talented (valuable) individuals. This means finding agreement (by both parties) on the equation's numerical value. Remembering they also have an intrinsic value that should also be considered but isn't germane to our discussion. Meaning going forward, as with any relationship, we can and are growing together. We're partners in the success of the venture. I grow, you grow, and we grow together. (Especially financially)

Some might argue though, a job, whether it pays weekly or every two weeks is not fast enough. I want faster earnings. Or I want more, larger earnings.
That's your decision.
Perhaps then, from my example you're the advertising board instead of the advertising host.

Again becoming an invaluable resource is essential. Take Craig's list for an example; employers will come to you, sellers can come to you. Buyers can come to you, people looking for jobs they all come to YOU.
You earn, they are your traffic. The point is, you have to be that invaluable resource. The key is the same. The goal is the same – getting paid! Where you are (in the equation) is where you see yourself. How you get there is determined by what you're trying to accomplish.

If that's not fast enough, continuing the example. You can then capitalize off the needs of others. Build your capital from a need or deficiency in others ability. If you're truly looking to make a fast buck, or make some money monetizing you - quickly. Then there is one sure way to get you paid.

They Won't but I Can

What others won't or can't do. Somebody will. Why not you?

Bill Money

Principle 5
The Drive - More Than Others Define

> *Whatever you find to do, do it well because where you are going—the grave—there will be no working or thinking or knowing or wisdom.*
> ECCLESIASTES 9:10 (VOICE)

Before engaging this last thought on the subject of monetizing me. I'd like to circle back for a moment to an idea introduced in an earlier thought. The idea of partnering and a social construct. Social media as an example is a great way and an easy way to partner (work together) and monetize yourself.

The same principles apply with one glaring exception. People never really get to know you. They know or discover the person you present. But the reality, more expressly, the value of your actual being is lost. In some cases even misappropriated. Don't however misunderstand my sentiments on the issue. Facebook, Twitter, tik-tok are valuable tools to use and important to the landscape of being useful - resources. But remember they are only instruments for the people behind them to make money monetizing you.

You want to make money, as I did, monetizing yourself. Feel free to use these tools as an avenue to build and even engage with perhaps your future partners. Because as the name implies social media is there to aid you in being social. To discover like minded individuals.

But that's not the end.

As a tool, social media or media in general can help you find a window from which to view varying levels and degrees of success. As a tool, it provides great resources and healthy benefits. However, the risk versus reward is important to weigh in your journey. As I said. The construct is not meant to display reality. It's meant as a reality. An alternative to render aid for some and a benefit for others. In my estimation it can be a kind of trojan horse. Meant to aid others in destroying you and your efforts. My advice here is be careful how you employ this particular tool!

Again though let's get back to building and collecting wealth. The best investment or strategy, to monetizing your efforts, is you. Answering the question, What am I willing to do?

We've invested in what you know and spent time in what's in your hand? Now let's have a look at what you can and specifically, will do!

From a media perspective you can use the platforms that exist or if you're skilled enough build your own. For me it's getting information to you which means writing and producing. Utilizing the tools I'm afforded. Strategically and purposefully that's one of the reasons you have this book. Regardless of whatever tool I use, the answer remains the same. Putting in the effort always yields results.

And that's what I can't overemphasize to you. Find what works - for you!

Bill Money

How do you do that, you might say?

I've got an idea.

[More]

The answer to what I'm willing to do for more is. Whatever it takes to have more!

For writers that means writing. For Builders that means building. Whatever your hand finds to do, DO IT! And with excellence I should add. There are countless opportunities to earn. The opportunity you take is as easy a decision as what makes you happy. What idea keeps you going when everything falls apart.

In fact, if it were me. I would even take things a step further. For expedience sake, I would add, what can you do that makes life easier for you and somebody else? Because I realize that we do age. And even though yardwork may not displease you when you're young. As you age, and it becomes more taxing, this includes the weather changes. You'll want to find something else to do that provides just as much joy. So why not start your mind on it now?

Put your mind to work for you now and you'll definitely

benefit later. This includes your efforts to find a worthy partner. This too becomes more difficult as we age. Yet I can't be adamant enough about this. Nothing will get you paid quicker than agreement. Nothing will boost your multiplication efforts faster and greater than agreement. Or rather as it's called, partnership.

That's the ultimate arbiter of what you're willing to do. Because the key to doing and being excellent is recognition of those who are excelling with you. Call them counselors or advisors. So often we don't see all we can do. We only see what we want. Others however have the gift of insight into us and what we demonstrate ourselves capable of. You've heard statements like "he/she can do whatever they put their minds to" whatever you put the mind to. Whatever you put thought and consideration on - the body will follow suit and perform.

What follows next is literal fruit. Tangible, edible, produce. All it takes is your willingness to work. Especially together.

And ultimately that's my goal in crafting this message, this book. I want us to enjoy the action of work. Enjoy the

The Drive To Monetize ME

benefits of work. Enjoy life in the fullest sense of being fruitful and multiplying.

Taking something somebody else won't do or even can't do can get you paid faster than anything on the planet. Because then you truly develop an invaluable service. Then, You truly make yourself an appreciable asset.

Again though, all that's required is effort.

You have to put forth the effort if you want to quickly monetize me (you).

In that vein, ask yourself what am I willing to do that others aren't or don't want to do. This is a quick way to find your inspiration and even your niche. If your goal is to advance into wealth building without all the learning and educating yourself. A wise man once told me. The answer's in the back of the book.

Just find something someone else doesn't (want to) or can't do. For the right personality this can be your ticket to great rewards. An easy and quite rewarding and profitable adventure. Plus it may even help you identify the thing in you you didn't know about yet. That hidden talent you haven't discovered yet. The unique ability you possess but haven't exercised yet. In the end that's what I think our focus is on. To gather wealth and financial certainty but also be happier and more content people. A preacher once said hurting people hurt people. I'll add, hurt people make the best healers as they have already been through the pain.

Regardless of which path you choose or whether you go a whole nother direction from my thoughts. There remains the possibility of enriching you and by extension, I mean me. This was something I had the benefit of learning before I was too old to do something about it. There are always tasks others aren't willing to do or even unable. The key to extreme wealth is doing them. I might add and do them well. Consider this. There are whole companies built around getting you food from fresh food and groceries to fast food. Who would have thought of this years ago. There is so much more opportunity to gain wealth beyond the traditional means. All it takes is somebody willing to examine themselves and put their idea to work for them.

May you or I be that someone!

Bill Money

Gratitude

Thank you for your investment in this publication and in me (the author) for the benefit of growing to present a better man to the world.

Also, please keep in mind this special verse.

Use all your strength to do the work that you are doing. One day you will die and you will go into your grave. Then you will not have any work, or ideas, or knowledge or wisdom. So do your work well while you are alive. ECC 9:10 (EASY)

More From 4FM Publishing

Available Today!

   Your Extraordinary Life Awaits

In "Humanity's Prowess," explore the profound truth of man's unique place in God's creation. This enlightening book delves into the sacred responsibilities bestowed upon us: to worship our Creator and to steward the earth with care and reverence.

Through compelling narratives, theological insights, and practical guidance, "Humanity's Prowess" illuminates the divine purpose and extraordinary role of mankind. Embrace your calling, deepen your faith, and learn to nurture the world as a reflection of God's love and God's magnificence. Discover the divine significance of your existence and the profound impact you can make on the human condition.

Biography

William "Bill" Money, a man whose name seemed predestined for financial gains, began his journey in the bustling corridors of the University of Southern California. Graduating with a degree in finance, Bill quickly ascended the ranks to become a respected financial adviser, guiding countless clients through the intricate dance of investments and wealth management.

A timely sabbatical led Bill to decide, rather, to embark on a new role apart from the world of finance, becoming a life coach and traveling minister. A role in which he's dedicated himself to helping others find not only financial stability but also spiritual and emotional fulfillment. His seminars and workshops have become a beacon of hope for many, blending practical life skills with deep, transformative spiritual insights.

Bill Money's journey from a financial expert to a life coach and evangelist reflects his profound belief that true wealth is measured not in dollars, but in the richness of one's spirit and relationships

From the Author –

"The reason so many of my writings are filled with biblical text and ideas is I'm a believer. I believe and accept that Christ died for me especially, for man. And writing to me is an expression of my faith."

www.ingramcontent.com/pod-product-compliance
Lightning Source LLC
Chambersburg PA
CBHW071409040426
42444CB00009B/2166